Community Helpers During COVID-19

Health Care Workers
During COVID-19

Robin Johnson

CRABTREE
PUBLISHING COMPANY
WWW.CRABTREEBOOKS.COM

CRABTREE
PUBLISHING COMPANY
WWW.CRABTREEBOOKS.COM

Author: Robin Johnson
Series research and development:
Janine Deschenes
Editorial director: Kathy Middleton
Editor: Janine Deschenes
Proofreader: Melissa Boyce
Graphic design: Katherine Berti
Image research: Robin Johnson
Print coordinator: Katherine Berti

Library and Archives Canada Cataloguing in Publication

Title: Health care workers during COVID-19 / Robin Johnson.
Names: Johnson, Robin (Robin R.), author.
Description: Series statement: Community helpers during COVID-19 |
   Includes index.
Identifiers: Canadiana (print) 20200390856 |
   Canadiana (ebook) 20200390864 |
   ISBN 9781427128331 (hardcover) |
   ISBN 9781427128379 (softcover) |
   ISBN 9781427128416 (HTML)
Subjects: LCSH: COVID-19 (Disease)–Juvenile literature. |
   LCSH: Medical personnel–Juvenile literature. |
   LCSH: Epidemics–Social aspects–Juvenile literature. |
   LCSH: Community life–Juvenile literature.
Classification: LCC RA644.C67 J643 2021 | DDC j610.69–dc23

Library of Congress Cataloging-in-Publication Data

Available at the Library of Congress

Crabtree Publishing Company

www.crabtreebooks.com   1-800-387-7650

Printed in the U.S.A./012021/CG20201112

**Published
in Canada**
Crabtree Publishing
616 Welland Ave.
St. Catharines, Ontario
L2M 5V6

**Published in the
United States**
Crabtree Publishing
347 Fifth Ave.
Suite 1402-145
New York, NY 10016

**Published in the
United Kingdom**
Crabtree Publishing
Maritime House
Basin Road North, Hove
BN41 1WR

**Published
in Australia**
Crabtree Publishing
Unit 3 - 5 Currumbin Court
Capalaba
QLD 4157

Contents

Dangerous Disease

In 2019, a **disease** called COVID-19 began to make people sick. Some people coughed or had trouble breathing. Some showed other signs they were sick. The disease spread quickly around the world. Soon it became a **pandemic**.

Doctors around the world are helping people who are sick from COVID-19.

Scientists studied COVID-19 to learn how to stop it from spreading. They said people should wash their hands often and try to stay home. If people had to go out, they should wear masks on their faces. They should not get too close to other people.

Many world leaders listened to scientists and made rules to keep people safe. Some leaders decided there should be a **lockdown** for a period of time. Schools and some businesses were shut down.

This helper is checking a boy's **temperature** to see if he is sick.

Community Care

Helpers in every community work together to care for people with COVID-19. A community is a group of people who live, work, and play in the same area. Hospitals and doctors' offices are part of communities.

Some communities do not have enough room in their hospitals. They set up tents so helpers can care for sick people.

It takes many health care workers to keep a hospital running.

People have a **basic need** to be cared for when they are sick. Brave health care workers make sure that need is met. They are workers who are trained to help sick and injured people.

People have been very thankful for health care workers during the pandemic!

Doctors

Doctors are helpers who figure out what is wrong with sick people. They ask **patients** questions. They look carefully at their bodies. Doctors have tests done and study the results. Then doctors tell patients what they need to do to get better.

> Doctors and other helpers work together to help people during the pandemic.

Doctors wear face masks, safety glasses, gloves, and suits to stay safe.

During the pandemic, doctors work long hours in crowded hospitals. They see many patients. Doctors wear special masks and other **equipment** so they do not spread COVID-19. They travel to the communities where people need help.

Doctors help some of their patients on the phone or online.

Nurses

Nurses work with doctors and other helpers to care for sick people. They ask patients questions to find out what is wrong. They take people's temperatures. They give patients medicine and help them get better.

Nurses test many people for COVID-19. Some people are tested right in their cars!

These nurses are checking on a patient with COVID-19.

Nurses have many new jobs during the pandemic. They test people for COVID-19 and explain the results. They answer questions on phone help lines. Nurses keep patients safely away from other people. They **comfort** patients who are very sick from the disease.

Patients are not allowed to have visitors during the pandemic. Nurses help them talk to their families.

Looking at Lungs

Some health care workers study people's lungs. Lungs are body parts in our chests that we use to breathe air. Some people with COVID-19 have problems with their lungs. Workers use machines to help them breathe.

Health care workers listen to the lungs of patients.

Health care workers use machines to help people breathe.

Other health care workers take X-rays. X-rays are pictures that show parts inside our bodies. Workers study X-rays of people's lungs to see if they have COVID-19. They use the X-rays to help patients get better.

This health care worker explains X-ray results to a patient.

Paramedics

Paramedics are health care workers who answer **emergency** calls. They travel quickly by **ambulance** to help people who are very sick or hurt.

These paramedics are taking a patient out of an ambulance.

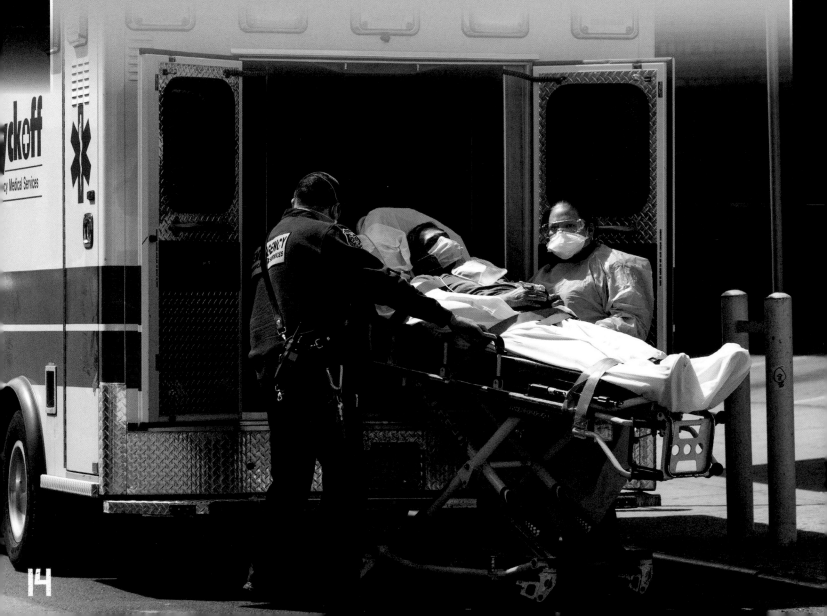

Paramedics look after people. They give them medicine. Then they rush patients to hospitals. Paramedics have responded to many calls during the pandemic. They wear masks and other safety equipment. They carefully clean ambulances.

*Workers in Mexico **designed** a cover so paramedics can carry patients safely.*

These paramedics took a patient to a hospital set up in a tent.

Care Each Day

Health care workers do not just help people in emergencies. Some help people with their needs each day. These workers might feed people or help them get dressed. They might give them medicine.

This health care worker is helping a boy exercise. These kinds of exercises help make people stronger.

During lockdowns, visitors were not allowed in many care homes where people live together. Helpers tried to keep people from feeling lonely.

This health care worker is checking a patient's heart at home.

Some health care workers visit people in their own homes. Others work in large care homes where many people live together. Workers try to keep COVID-19 from spreading through the homes. They clean carefully and keep people safely apart.

17

Mental Health Workers

Many people have felt scared, sad, or lonely during the pandemic. Some people are afraid they will get sick. Many have to stay away from their families and friends. Workers help people deal with their feelings and improve their **mental** health.

Children need mental health support too.

Many people worry about their own health, their loved ones getting sick, or losing their jobs. Mental health workers make sure they have someone to talk to.

Mental health workers listen to people and show them they are not alone.

Many mental health workers talk to people on the phone and online. They listen carefully. Then, they give people ideas to help them feel better. Workers also post tips online so people can get help whenever they need it.

Other Health Helpers

It takes many workers to give people the care they need. Some workers keep track of information about a patient's health. Others carefully clean hospitals. Some workers make repairs to keep hospitals safe. They are all busy during the pandemic.

It takes many workers to keep hospitals clean and safe.

Animals need care during the pandemic too! Animal doctors called vets take good care of dogs, cats, and other pets. They give them medicine and help keep them healthy and happy.

This vet is taking good care of a sick dog.

This worker is repairing a machine in a hospital.

Glossary

ambulance A vehicle used to carry sick or injured people

basic need Something that people cannot live without

comfort To make someone feel less sad or scared

designed Made a plan for how something is made or built

disease A sickness that prevents a person's body from working as it should

emergency An unexpected event that needs quick action

equipment Supplies or tools needed for a special purpose

lockdown A rule for people to stay where they are

mental Having to do with a person's mind

pandemic A disease spreading over the whole world or a very wide area, such as many countries

patient A person who gets care from a health care worker

scientists People who study and have a lot of knowledge about science

temperature A measure of how hot or cold something is

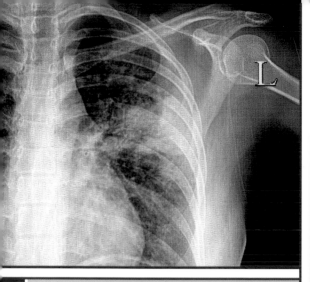

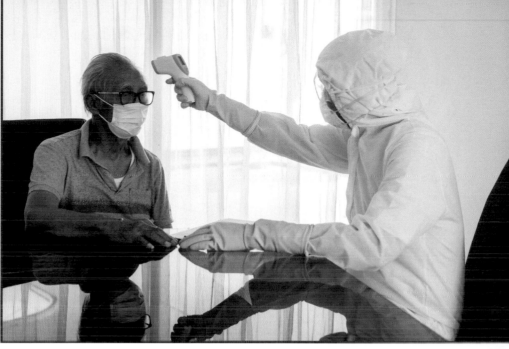

Index

About the Author

Robin Johnson is a freelance author and editor who has written more than 100 published children's books. She was fortunate to work from home during the pandemic and is grateful to all the helpers who kept her community running and her family safe.

Notes to Parents and Educators

Health Care Workers During COVID-19 celebrates the brave health care workers who are helping members of their communities stay safe, receive daily care, and meet their basic need for health care. Below are suggestions to help children make connections and develop their reading and social studies skills.

Before reading

Read the title of the book to children. Create a K-W-L chart and fill in the first column: What Do I **K**now? Ask children:

- Who are health care workers? What jobs do they do?

During reading

After reading pages 4 and 5, fill in the second column of the chart: What Do I **W**ant To Know? Ask children:

- What do you want to know about how health care workers are helping others during COVID-19?

After reading

Fill in the third and final column of the chart: What Did I **L**earn? Ask children:

- What jobs do health care workers do during COVID-19?

- How did the jobs of health care workers change because of COVID-19?

Invite children to write down a question they still have about how health care workers help others during COVID-19. Investigate answers together.